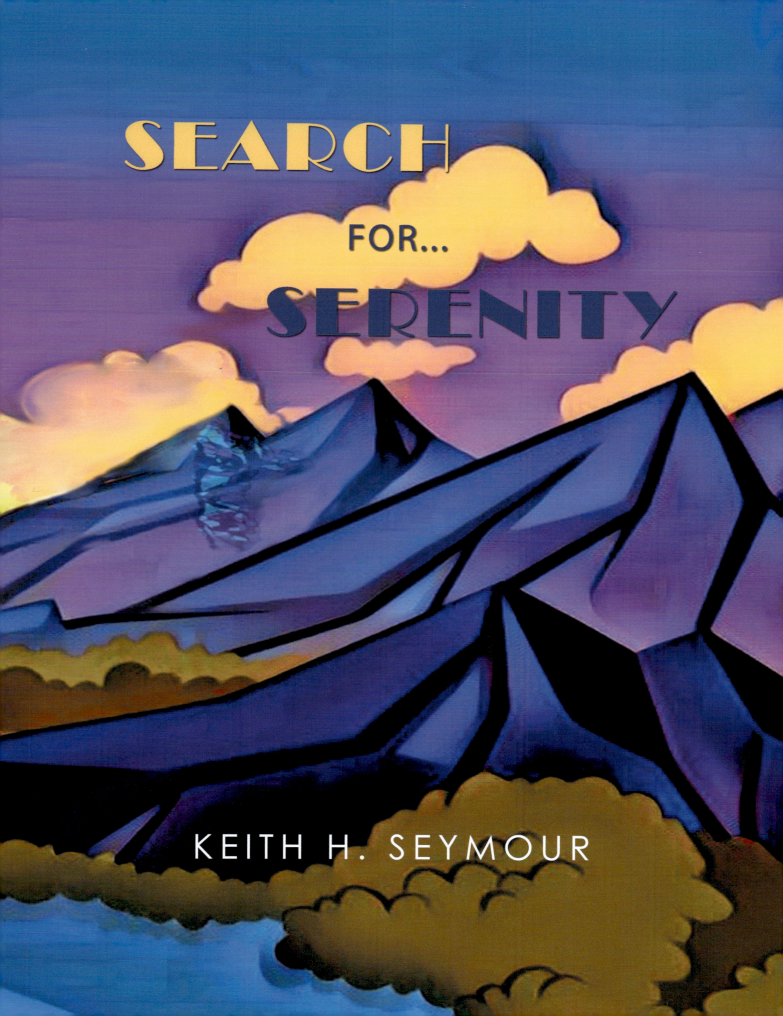

SEARCH

FOR...

SERENITY

KEITH H. SEYMOUR

Print information available on the last page

Rev. date: 06/27/2018

SEARCH FOR.....SERENITY

Poems by

Keith H. Seymour

To order additional copies of this book, contact:
Xlibris
1-888-795-4274
www.Xlibris.com
Orders@Xlibris.com

ACKNOWLEDGEMENTS

While it is true that the writer creates the manuscript, it is also true that there is a support system for each writer that is key in the inspiration and support of that author, and the creation of the work. I would therefore be remiss in not acknowledging the following people people for their important contributions.

I searched literally for years for an illustrator who could understand and cooperate with me. Finally, I had the good luck to come across Ms. Lisa Viera a local artist, and owner of "Blue Buttery Galleries." Lisa actually read my poems and came up with a vision for my art. After two or three days, Lisa came up with the cover art, Elements of which are used as background for the poems. Lisa you are truly an "Artistic Genius." I would not be able to have put this book out without you.

My Production and marketing staff at Xlibris publishing. Particularly Cheryl Ishigaki, Marketing Consultant William Stein, and the rest of of their staff. Your help and patience has been paramount in the creation of this book. Marami Salamat Po. (Much Thanks!). I also need to thank my family, friends, and the members of my "Mind Gravy" poetry group.

Much thanks to these and countless of other people who have been of such great assistance to me in each and every aspect of this book's creation.

Keith H. Seymour
"Search for.. Serenity"

Contents

The Rivers

Just as the water
Of each and every river
flows
over and through
each pebble, stone, and grain of sand
that lies within its path,
So do all of our lives.
As they flow.
They travel
over and throughout time.

Yet, as those rivers begin their travels
that will guide
them into
their intended destinies,
they know not of where, how and when
their journeys will end.

Yet,
a special grace will flow throughout each one's
Special.... and unique existence.
An existence
maintained as each river looks to God's guiding hand,
In leading them to the promised truths
That lay ahead for them to discover.

In much the same way,
mortals also look to God
through each multi-coloured horizon,
each sun, each moon, each star,
and each day and evening
still yet to come.

These special gifts from above
Guide and protect us

as we search for...
those eternal truths and destinies
That only
God
holds and guides us toward
with His gentle and embracing touch.

Therefore,
just as each and every river is created
in a manner, that allows it
to overcome each pebble and stone,
So is each and very mortal created
to overcome
each unexpected obstacle that is presented
along life's various paths.

It is these same paths and obstacles
That makes us
who and what we were, are,
and yes...who and what we will become.
The beautiful and unique creations-
molded by the perfect and parental hands
that will someday
help us to understand and appreciate
each and every discovered destiny.

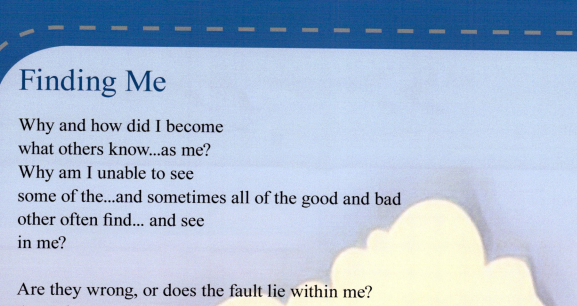

Finding Me

Why and how did I become
what others know...as me?
Why am I unable to see
some of the...and sometimes all of the good and bad
other often find... and see
in me?

Are they wrong, or does the fault lie within me?
Am I the tree within my own forest,
or am just on a journey...blindly searching
for me?

Paradox

Where do I fit in?
Why am I here?
The fact is,
I fit in everywhere
and nowhere.
People notice me
when I am gone,
but rarely when I am present!
The people closest to me
know me the least.
Whereas those .. .. *unknown caring individuals ...*
even strangers,
know me the best.
Am I the proverbial forest for the trees
that cannot be seen ... even though I am there?
The sound of a mighty redwood
fallen
but possibly never heard?
If so,
doesn't that make me human
like everyone else,,,or something
less?
Shouldn't I also be asking these questions
of everyone I know
and especially....those I don't?
Maybe the problem is not necessarily how others see me,
but how I see others ... and ... me.
So where do I fit in,
and why am I here
if
I fit no where ... and concurrently
everywhere?

Un-Rest

A peace of the world,
and therefore,
A piece of me ...
is rudely awakened by
anger, greed, fear, and ignorance.
Causing ... individual and universal conflict.
For a piece disturbed is a peace no more.
Especially since ...
Well, my world is so troubled
That it so often claims to fight for a peace
So universally and mutually humane."
Yet with itself... it seems to be
Constantly
at War.

STANDING STILL

Why do I stand here,
remaining in the same place?
Even though I move,
I never seem to leave
this spot... this place.
If remaining does not work.. I leave.
If leaving does not work...I stay.
I travel... inside the box, outside the box.
And everywhere else in between.
I continually travel to and through
every geometrical, geographical,
physiological area and variable
As well my own spirit-uality.
I am consistently,
the confused traveler... and permanent resident.
I just wish I knew
why I constantly move... and yet
I am always here... standing still.
Even though I obviously
catch up with and often times... surpass
the others,
their lives move forward while mine remains...stagnant..
The definition of insanity:
"Doing the same thing,
even though the method is proven not to work."
So after discovering what does not work for me,
and discovering what does work,
Why does my life... not work for me?
Why do I go insane
trying to figure out the reason
I remain... in the same place?
Why do I always find myself and my life
standing still?

THE BUSY ME...OR WE!!!

They say to me,
"You certainly keep busy!"
I merely reply:
You have to
in this day and time!
They smile, laugh, or both
and say:
Amen! I hear that! I know what you mean.

They say to many
"You certainly keep busy!"
I just smile and think:
I wish!
If they only knew the truth.
Is is...Just God and me.
And sometimes, HE seems absent
even though... I know HE isn't.
Still, no close mortal acquaintance.
It;s just me.

I keep so busy,
because....I'm not.

I keep so busy
because there is nothing to do,
or anyone with which to do it.

People often... are so busy
to hide loneliness and boredom
from others
and me.

They tell you and me,
"you are always so busy!"
They say that
because
that is what we allow them to see.

Yes, I always stay busy.
That pretense is how
I comfortably survive
and remain..or hide the real me.

UN-I-DENTIFIED

I enter a seemingly familiar room... or place.
Sometimes it is a function to which... I have been invited,
or of which they have made me...
A part.
And though the people there seen to notice me...
They really don't.
They say hello
and ask about my health...
Always asking about... some person or acquaintance
we currently know, or at least... we once mutually knew.
Their words and expressions
that flow with continuous consistency
seem to indicate
some sort of acknowledgment of me.
Yet, the tone in their voices
and their eyes... Oh their blank eyes...
They all say something else.
I would not say it is like... I'm invisible
to... them.
It is more that... Even though I know
I am here,, to everyone else
I don't really exist
and never...Really did.

Faces

We all wear faces, several different faces.

We wear them ... Concurrently and at different times.

We all wear faces, different faces.

Not masks, for masks hide what is really there.

Whereas, our various faces

actually exhibit what is sometimes ... maybe often

truly not seen by ourselves ... or others.

Not roles ... not parts we play in our lives .... but faces of the whole

faces that fill .... and sometimes create

voids.

We all wear faces, many different faces

that show sides, parts, each portion of our entire being.

These faces are both good and bad.

Sometimes we recognize them ... sometimes not.

Sometimes remembered ... by others, sometimes forgot.

We all wear faces. Yes! We all wear several different faces.

Just because we may not recognize them when present, does not mean they are not there.

Just because others do not see them, does not mean for us they truly don't care.

We all wear faces. Yes, we all wear faces.

Some discovered, some still hidden.

I have them, and so do you.

We often find out about them, when we least expect to.

These faces are never false, and though they sometimes exhibit our faults,

they are still "apparently" true.

The problem of mere mortals finding out we have so many faces,

is that

we are often surprised as discovering how, when, where, and why they show up.

Oftentimes causing us to question who were are, and why we're here.

Yes, we all wear many faces, that whether we know it or not,

are always with us. They are always there.

Private Fences

Some-one
once observed:
good neighbors
are created by, good fences.
Many who find warmth
within this "Frosty" cliché
point out that
these barriers
may be enhanced or lessened
based upon what the architect or owner
wishes to prove
is exclusively owned,
needs to be protected, or kept private
from others.
Even including
in some cases....those wishing to control
a certain amount
of
intimacy... that may be shared.
These private fences strengthen the strong,
and alienate the weak.
They protect certain individuals
from those...deemed unworthy, dishonest,
or those that merely make us feel uncomfortable
because they are different... worse!
More like us
in subtle ways, we can't or won't admit.
So, while many fences are legitimately built
to protect all that has been built and earned through hard work,
others are built, as a result of people
working hard to protect themselves not just from others.
But themselves.
Many architects and owners of these fences,
build such barriers to guard...other fences
revealing
a more vulnerable place
They don't want... their neighbors, fellow humans to see.

The Unidentifiable Feeling

What's this feeling that I do not know?
What is it that I actually feel,
This unidentifiable feeling
I need to heal?
Tis not pain, pleasure, or numbness either.
All I know, is that when I experience it,
It seems like I am experiencing
The "world of nether."
If a brave man seeks knowledge
At the risk of being hurt,
And a wise man avoids
Unhappiness and hurt
At the risk of becoming a fool,
What does a man who wishes
To be a man of both wisdom and valor do?
Especially if he knows that he "must" choose
between the two.
Do I choose between being a coward or a fool?
A brave idiot, or a wise coward?
If I am unable to identify this feeling,
How may I go forward?
All I really know is that when I feel this way,
I always wish that from my life
It would immediately sever.
Instead of waiting for it to disappear.
Which seems like forever!

HOME

I accidentally glanced at the sunset the other day.
and ever since,
I've thought of you... of home.
The green grass of Spring, the glorious smell of food,
the recently illuminated lights that coloured the river...
even the sounds of people celebrating
didn't keep my attention.
Yet, the accidental view of the sunset did.
You see, it made me think of home. It made me think of you.
You see... I was, and am at home.
I'm in a place so native and familiar to me,
that I know it all too well.
It wasn't until I met you
that this place
began to cause me such loneliness and pain.
You see... you are not here, but in some other place
that I may not currently go to.
But my heart can... and more often than not
does.
So, if home is where the heart is,
I am not really home.
For my heart is with you, and it is merely my physical being
that is here.
Unfortunately, you aren't.
So, while my heart is at home... with you,
the rest of me
isn't.

Presently me

I have known future. There *will* be *nothing* there.
I have known past. There has never been
anything ... for me.
Only the present.. .is *all* I know ... as existing for me.
The people I *have* loved ... and who have loved me,
no longer exist ... and never *have*.
Those whom I will/love ... and who *will* love me,
are unknown, and will remain so ... to me.
The people with whom I presently share
mutual affection. .. are only temporary
and
really don't... truly exist.
This ... *apparent* truth is not because people from my past
are no longer here.
For no *true* past is traceable to me.
Neither, is it because ... people presently
known to be in my life, will someday ... *no longer be.*
Since ... no future ... is cognizant of me.
You see, if the truth is that the future is now,
those *presently* in my life
are not really now ... or ever will be
here or there.
For in the future ... in some form or time
they will leave.
Logically then, *I must conclude*
that I may only *now* ... depend on the person
known as me,
I am *now* ... the only one to whom my feelings
can be
exposed, shared, explored, resolved.
I must go on alone ... and forever depend only upon myself
myself
now and here . .. anytime ... anywhere.

THE DIALOUGE

I am so tired of...this conversation.
So stop opposing me!!!
It is after all,
my happiness and productivity
at stake here.

you're right...
you don't understand... and never really have.
But only because you... never really tried.
No! You haven't!
So don't tell me that you have!
If you had,
We would not be having this conversation.. Again.
Only this time,
why don't you just shut up and listen to me!
You may actually become enlightened.
Okay?
Okay.

For once, I need to give to, and be happy
with me.
I need to find my niche'
in a place
that will make me happy.
Rather than....always living up to some dictate
created by society
No, I can't do that in this place.
Why?
Well, I just feel like...
No! Do not inter-rupt me.
You're wrong. I don't feel like an oddly shaped piece
that is constantly attempting to fit into
an otherwise correct, yet puzzling world.
It is more like...
being... an unaccepted, but correct puzzle

constantly trying to fit into
some incorrect and detached entity

I am so tired of feeling this way,
and I know this will not change.
At lease...
as long as I remain
in this current place.

I said stop it!
Do not lec-ture me.
I've been myself. It didn't work.
Don't tell me to conform and compromise.
I've done that too.
No! When I did that,
I was no longer labeled a misfit... just a hypocrite
by others...and you.
All because I did what was best for you.
Yet. You never did what was best for me.

I know.
I know you're sorry to see me leave.
My presence is paramount to your survival.
But your survival means my defeat.

Oh I am being silly, you say?
Well, if I don't need to change my life and thinking,
If I am wrong about you...
Answer me one question.
Why do I argue with myself
about something, that I know
I must do.

A want to Feel

I want to feel.. .. I want to *feel* something special!
I want to feel like,
I have made a *positive* difference
somewhere, at sometime, for somebody..anybody,
and still do.
I want to feel or have Faith of something special...
even if I am not sure that it is there.
Don't apologize, because you think you have offended me
when I have given no such indication.
That makes me feel,
as if I made you feel insecure...
or someone else has,
and you see me as no better.
I want you to feel secure about me ...as a friend, a person, a human being,
a mere mortal.
I want you to feel and know that you are a special person.
Not just to me, but to others, and more importantly
to GOD.

I don't just want to feel like a valued employee, friend, or family member.
I want to feel like...you know I will listen when you need an ear,
I will be your heart, when you need a reason to care, or your strength
when you are too tired to try.
I want to feel like you know that... I actively and sincerely care.

I want to feel... like you believe I am worth the effort
of reminding me
that there is a green pasture over the next mountain or hill,
even when all my hopes and dreams ...seemed to have faded and disappeared,
and I have lost all hope... that any will ever again appear.
I want to feel... that I am so special to you...you refuse to let me give up
on me...you.. us...anything!

I do not want to feel like an obligation, or something
you have gotten used to over time,

the way someone gets used to an unwanted present they feel too guilty to exchange,
or an elderly relative or friend who has your respect
due to their advanced age.
I want to feel like... even with all my failures and frailties
you are proud to have me as part of your past, present, and future.

Maybe the sun did not shine any brighter because I was in your life another day.
Or the moon and the stars had no more majestic a glow,
because you ended your day, knowing I was a part of it.
Still,
like anyone else,
I just need to feel... like I have... and do
make a positive difference
to you...somebody...at sometime..someplace... somewhere.

Sighting ... the Truth

If we were blind...and touched
the other's
hands, eyes, face, or any other part....of our physical being,.
how would we know... the hue, shade or color
of the other's skin?
Unless....
somehow... verbally.... revealed.
It is therefore, not what we see with the eyes placed within in our heads
that matters,
but the eyes from within ... and that express our true selves.
The eyes placed within our hearts ... our souls.
I do not know .... whether or not there would be
less
fear, hate, prejudice, or war
if the world population *suddenly* lost the ability of *physical sight*
or even
If God in his wisdom, had never endowed mortals with this gift.
Therefore, forcing mortals to use the *eyes from within,*
we would be more apt to love .. .instead of hate.-
I only know
that *true blindness* .... *comes not* from loss of physical sight
but.
The inability ... or refusal
to see others *and ourselves* ... using the eyes placed within
our hearts and souls.

The Truth

I used to believe
That
it was my fault
That you feel about me
The *way-that you do!*
I thought ... I *deserved* the fact
That you couldn't... no, wouldn't deal with me.
Well, maybe at first
That might have been true.
But Now?
You are just being petty and cruel.
Now, I'm the one who's making all efforts
o make this relationship work.
So go ahead... write me off as worthless.
I don't care! I know better!
But I won't be written off or used as:
"your patsy, scapegoat, or fool."
I will no longer
Feel bad because
You're
a gutless coward.
So you don't have the guts
to say that you
resent me... for being in your life?
A fact that... may be changed
Only by death.
Then again,
Possibly not even that,
unless one of us goes to a far worse place.
I'm comfortable with my soul.
Can you say the same about yours?
That is assuming
You actually have one.
Don't worry.

I am not wishing that you go
to a place that is not so nice.
I wouldn't give you the pleasure.
Actually, I'm hoping that we both end up
in the same pleasant location.
Then you'll have to deal with me!
Upon command from
A much higher
Authority.
Meanwhile,
just say that you wish for me
to be out of your life.
Say it!
No, you won't say it. I know you.
you're too much of a coward.
you may not care now,
But just remember,
that our acquaintance... Karma
will behave like one' hell of a bitch
when she visits you, on behalf of me.
You see, someday
you will need me, unconditionally.
Just as I once needed you,
When you continually refused to aid to me.
When that day happens...
 And it will...
don't forget to ask yourself
if you truly... deserve my assistance.
Because...
Whether I give it or not
We'll both know
The Truth!

Stepping out of the Shadows

I won't live there anymore!
It is not conducive to the positive environment
that I wish for my soul.
I will not remain,
regardless of how difficult it is for me to leave.
No! I will no longer allow
you, others, and more importantly
myself
to measure my worth, or that of my
accomplishments
by some image that has been generated by another.
There was a time when I consciously...
and unconsciously
did this on the illusion
that... this image was
safe.
As a result, I didn't even become...a person
living within the shadow of another person.
Rather, I became merely a shadow
residing within the shadow of another shadow.
It seems... that at some point, I surrendered
my
personage
by allowing my beauty, worth, and accomplishments
to become engulfed by what others and I perceived
as the existence of the past, present, and future
of, well...
you and your accomplishments...
and even
those of others.
Therefore, I was always afraid,
that my shadow
would never become as great as yours.
Then, something
caused me to step outside of ...your shadow.

At that very moment,
the sun began to lovingly shine
more upon my accomplishments
and yes,
my shortcomings-both big and small.
Oddly enough, I was no longer scared.
Maybe because I had begun to
more willingly take responsibility?
I don't know.
I just know it feels good to focus
on my accomplishments, and even my shortcomings
Rather than worrying about yours.

CHOOSING TO LIVE IN A WORLD THAT-

I once heard a song...
from
what is now known
as the ... "Baby Boom Era.".
The song's refrain,
"I won't live in a world without love"
is oh still so clear to me!
So, I now wonder,
has that... same generation,
once known for proselytizing
this ideal of the world,
now exchanged
the values of love, understanding, and compassion
with those of
status, established power, and wealth?
I recently had a conversation with a longtime acquaintance.
An esteemed and prosperous old Black man,
A product of that era, and once known
to espouse...and live
the ideals of that song's refrain.
As we spoke of tragic events occurring throughout the world,
he suddenly
sincerely proclaimed:
"Those people in the ninth ward of Louisiana,
those killed by Tsunamis, and those in poor wretched people in Haiti,
are all poor, desperate and lazy.
God gave them land to be productive and free!
It is because they aren't, they are, now
experiencing is God's wrath.
So, what has occurred, is as it must be.
Still, I will lend my aid to better their cause
because next year
it is a tax write off
for me."
I replied to his words abruptly, with an overtly offending glare

True, people need to pull themselves up by their bootstraps.
But what if they have no boots to wear?
Sure, if you teach a man to fish, he will eat for a lifetime,
but what if the source of that fish is poisoned,
and eating it
will not help sustain life, but rather...kill?
Then sir, I maintain that your proclamation
goes against... to GOD'S will.
Yes. I know, no true earthly Utopia will ever exist.
Yet, shouldn't we still strive to maintain ...a world in which
someone with an extra pair, will selflessly provide
the boots and the straps
to pull up and wear, and where people acknowledge
that poisoned fish is useless as food?.
No! I refuse to live in a world without love.
So the fact that I choose to remain...well it must mean
That somewhere in this world there still must be
others working to emphasize the greatest gifts
of
Faith, Hope, and Charity.

The Familiar Stranger

I met a stranger recently,
his presence ...
hard to ignore
I recognized this stranger,
as if *we'd* met before.
I recognized his features:
his face, his form,
and even the way he wore *his* hair.
Yet, as to *our* specific *meeting,*
I recalled not when or where!
So I decided I'd been mistaken,
or *our acquaintance was* long ago.
Also concluding,
surely *this individual*
was too unimportant
Even for me to ever know.
He appeared again later
and it really bothered
that this *seemingly* trivial person
was once ever known to mel?
Who was this person
whose image within *my* mind
was embedded so very deep?
Who was this individual
constantly *haunting* my waking hours,
and so *often* times ... *My sleep!*
My Answer?
I decided that if we had met before,
acknowledging *ambitions* and *obligations*
was *the far more important chore.*
So finally, I told him,
"Look later I'll deal with you.
Right now I have *more important people to patronize,*
and far more important things to dol"
So why he continued to bother me,

I had not the slightest clue
Then, after his appearances persisted
over a period of...
well, some great length
I suddenly recognized... his enviable characteristics
of serenity, confidence, and deep inner-strength.

It was only then
that this familiar stranger
chose to reveal himself to me
Stating: Aren't you yet aware?

I am no stranger that you see.
Rather, I am...
what we now know as
that self-neglected part of...
ME."

IT IS TIME....

It is time ...
It is time to let go.
It is not healthy to hang onto people and things
who
are disappearing, no longer wish to be a part of your life, or both.
I am not giving up ...
or giving in.
It is not within me ... to do so.
I am just
finally ...
giving to my self a little ... no a lot
of self-deserved peace.
Childhood memories...both good and bad,
childhood pranks, both given, but mostly received,
life's disappointments, betrayals, hurts...and oh yes!
All that angst!
Need no longer,,, and never should have been
such a dominant part of my life..nor should they be part
of
anyone else's life... ever again!
Yes, I know they will always to some degree remain within my mind
and a portion of the soul that makes me
who I am.
I know they will unexpectedly return from time to time,
as if they were...
rusty and cob webbed old cogs that spontaneously
and unexpectedly begin to cause the mind's windmills
to a speed that will need to be managed and over time
comfortably controlled
So, no matter how difficult or painful it may be,
it is time...time to look beyond the past and even the future,
in order to find the present.
In order to find
me.

The Meaning of Freedom

What is Freedom?
Tis' not a person, place, thing,
or an adjective,,, describing the same.
Or... is it?

What is Freedom?
Is it defined by a person, country, culture
of
the precepts held... therein?
After all, one person or culture's rigidness
could be
another's flexibility.

With freedom comes... the enslavement of responsibility
and therefore...rules.
Yet, when freedom is created by a majority
it may..oftentimes
inhibit and infringe upon the rights of the minority.
Such as...slavery.

Then again, If I were not free, and therefore
unable to define and recognize the same;
I should not be able to define... slavery.
Unless
I some how felt my liberties....were being enslaved
by
others.....or me!

If I define freedom as... what makes me happy,
and completes
my soul.
Yet, that same freedom makes others...
Especially those I love most,
frightened, angry, or unhappy,
what do I.... do?

Do... I
give up... that freedom
because
I somehow...equate their happiness with mine.
Or
do I selfishly create my freedom and happiness
even though
those about whom I care
may be saddened, frightened, or angry?

Must I sacrifice their approval or blessing,
to be blessed with my own freedom... my own happiness?
Such a choice to be free....enslaves my soul.

Maybe... freedom means
knowing myself...so to others I may be true.
However, what if I don't know myself,
or having others...even myself
know the real me...is something I am afraid to do?

On the other hand,
even if I knew myself, and was honest
with others about what I know to be freedom that is happy and true,
would it really matter?
Especially, if the meaning of true freedom
might be
different for me..and you.

Freedom Flight

The soul's spirit is like
a bird that does fly free
above, in a cloudy sky
of a blue and white sea.
The song of it's freedoms,
it so passionately sings,
while flying alongside
adventures most glorious wings.
The soul's spirit
may fly
to the moon, then its
destined star.
It may lead us to mysteries
near to home and heart,
or even to possibilities of the heart
somewhere afar.
When the soul's freedom flight
successfully flies to its highest peak,
a peaceful existence is eventually found.
Which is something each mortal does seek.

The Reachable Star

As I see the first star of the evening
resting upon the colors of dusk,
I see the star that is for me!

She shine as if she were hope
displayed
so far above
the trees, mountains, beaches, and hills,
where she delicately guards all passions
relating to.... my past and future dreams.
Sustaining...the glorious love that her creator
has commissioned her...to create and maintain
over hill, dale,, valley, and all the moonlit seas.

She is the star
of luxurious colors that glow
after a day's harshness and toil.
Her everlasting glow
is a symbol of triumphs trophy,
showing proud perseverance
and each beautifully redeeming quality
of humanity and nature,

My dreams and hopes, and even my fears
are all contained within that glittering
first... evening star,
that has not... and will not
fade or perish from my life.

Whether it is night or day,
my faith in my star... my guide
no person or force may alter.
For it is my star's faith in me
that I know will never cease or falter.

Serenity

I sat beside the ocean,
and looked upon a place
of God's creation that is...
So "perfectly" glorious to me!
A wonderful sight- the sunset ocean.
A calming image
of solid sandy specks of land,
and an exciting fluid mass of water,
Uniting,
In a marriage of
Serenity.

As the colours of dusk shone upon
the new grayish ocean,
I know that their warmth
benefited all of the sea's inhabitant's.
It was just then that I noticed:
The stillness of the land...
The silent ripple of the now peaceful sea.
Causing me to believe:
"that God had stopped time
Just for me."

As the sun and light
later began to completely fall,
the quietness of the ocean's being
spoke volumes to my spirit.
A spirit that...overflows
as I am permitted to humbly adore
the grace and beauty
of the most
glorious, exciting, and mysterious female of all

I will always love my ocean,
and she will always be precious to me.
Whether blue by day,
or deep black by night.
Whether she is brightened by the sun,
or a host of stars
her beauty will always be
"My very own"
Serenity.